Information about the author

Dr. Julie Meeson is an independent consulta[...] auditing, training and implementation of Q[...]ity Syst[...] experience in Clinical Research, with more t[...] [...] 10 years [...]ent in increasingly senior roles within Quality Assurance. She has worked for several major pharmaceutical companies and internation[...] [...] Research Organisations (CROs) and now runs her o[...] [...]nt Systems (www.j3iquality.com).

Withdrawn

Oct' 18

For Sale Scp

Directive 2001/20/EC of the European Parliament and of the council of 4 April 2001 on the approximation of the laws, regulations and administrative provisions of the Member States relating to the implementation of good clinical practice in the conduct of clinical trials on medicinal products for human use.

The Directive can be downloaded from the Internet:

http://europa.eu.int/eur-lex/pri/en/oj/dat/2001/l_121/l_12120010501en00340044.pdf

Abbreviations

ADR	Adverse Drug Reaction
AE	Adverse Event
CTA	Clinical Trial Authorisation
CTD	Clinical Trial Directive
DMC	Data Monitoring Committee
EEA	European Economic Area
EVCTM	Eudravigilance Clinical Trial Module
EVPM	Eudravigilance Postmarketing Module
EMEA	European Medicines Agency
GCP	Good Clinical Practice
GMP	Good Manufacturing Practice
ICH	International Conference on Harmonisation
IEC	Independent Ethics Committee
IMP	Investigational Medicinal Product
IMPD	Investigational Medicinal Product Dossier
MedRA	Medical Dictionary for Regulatory Activities Terminology
SAE	Serious Adverse Event
SmPC	Summary of Product Characteristics
SUSAR	Suspected, Unexpected, Serious Adverse Reaction
WMA	World Medical Association

Contents

Introduction

The Clinical Trial Directive 2001/20/EC and associated guidance documents provide the most extensive changes in the European Union clinical trial legislation for many years. This publication is intended to provide a summary of the key aspects of these documents. It must be emphasised that the full texts should be read, and referenced when important aspects of the process require elucidation. However, this booklet provides a useful overview of these extensive documents.

Chapter 1 - Introduction to Directive 2001/20/EC

Development of the CTD

The European Directive 2001/20/EC, commonly referred to as 'The Clinical Trial Directive' (CTD) began its official development in 1995 when it was issued as a concept paper. Following the first submission of the draft directive to the European Parliament and Council of Ministers in September 1997, an amended text went for its first reading at the European Parliament in Strasbourg in November 1998. Following several further rounds of consultation and amendments the CTD was eventually adopted by the European Commission in February 2001, and published in the Official Journal of the European Communities on 1st May 2001[1].

Implementation of the CTD

From the publication of the CTD each Member State had 2 years to review its existing clinical trial legislation and revise/supplement where necessary (Article 23). There was then a 1-year period to allow implementation of the new/revised local legislation, meaning that each Member State was expected to be fully compliant with the new CTD requirements by 1 May 2004. Whilst some Member States did achieve this deadline many did not, and only applied the new legislation after this.

Why is 2001/20/EC needed?

To help understand the need for the CTD it is useful to overview the regulatory environment with respect to clinical trials. Directive 2001/83/EC[2] (amended by 2004/27/EC[3]) is the principal reference document with respect to medicinal products and authorisation requirements. This piece of legislation is a 'codified' Directive, which means it draws together all the separate historical legislation that started with the 'grandfather' of medicinal legislation: Directive 65/65/EC[4]. However, there are very few references made to conducting clinical trials within 2001/83/EC[2]. Thus, in the absence of any pan European legislation governing how clinical trials should be conducted, national legislation was developed over the years within each Member State, which led to significant differences as to how clinical trials were conducted and controlled across Europe. Some of these differences meant that it was easier and/or quicker to initiate and conduct clinical trials in some Member States than others. This was not felt to be beneficial for a common unified approach across the European Union. The intent of the CTD was to introduce a 'level playing field' with respect to the rules and regulations relating to conduct of clinical trials, such that competition across the Member States within Europe was fairer. Another fundamental objective of the CTD was to ensure that adequate protection for human subjects in clinical trials was provided with a strong legal basis.

Objectives of the CTD

The formal objectives of the CTD can be summarised as follows:

- To ensure that only clinical trials with an acceptable risk:benefit assessment are conducted.

- To ensure that clinical trials are conducted according to Good Clinical Practice (GCP).

- To ensure medicinal products used in clinical trials are manufactured according to Good Manufacturing Practice (GMP).

- To harmonise and increase transparency of the administrative procedures for conduct of clinical trials.

- To reduce delays in starting clinical trials.

- To establish GCP and GMP inspection procedures.

- To create a repository for information on clinical trials conducted in the European Union.

- To establish fundamental ethical conduct within the legislation of the European Union.

- To provide special protection for vulnerable patients unable to give informed consent.

Chapter 2 - Overview of the CTD

Introduction

The CTD consists of twenty-four Articles, which are listed below. Full information on all of these topics can be found within the later sections of this publication.

- Preamble
- Article 1 – Scope
- Article 2 – Definitions
- Article 3 – Protection of trial subjects
- Article 4 – Clinical trials on minors
- Article 5 – Clinical trials on incapacitated adults not able to give informed legal consent
- Article 6 – Ethics Committees
- Article 7 – Singe opinion
- Article 8 – Detailed guidance
- Article 9 – Commencement of a clinical trial
- Article 10 – Conduct of a clinical trial
- Article 11 – Exchange of information
- Article 12 – Suspension of the trial or infringements
- Article 13 – Manufacture and import of investigational medicinal products
- Article 14 – Labelling
- Article 15 – Verification of compliance of investigational medicinal products with good clinical   and manufacturing practices
- Article 16 – Notification of adverse events
- Article 17 – Notification of adverse reactions
- Article 18 – Guidance concerning reports
- Article 19 – General provisions
- Article 20 – Adaptation to scientific and technical progress
- Article 21 – Committee procedure
- Article 22 – Application
- Article 23 – Entry into force
- Article 24 - Addresses

Scope and Applicability of the CTD

The CTD is applicable to all interventional clinical trials using a medicinal product, as defined within the definitions section. Both commercial and non-commercial clinical trials are within the scope of the new legislation. However, non-interventional trials are outside of the scope, with a non-interventional trial defined as a study where the medicinal product(s) are prescribed in the usual manner in accordance with the terms of the marketing authorisation; the assignment of the patient to a particular therapeutic strategy is not decided in advance by a trial protocol, but falls within current practice and the prescription of the medicine is clearly separated from the decision to include the patient in the study; no additional diagnostic or monitoring procedures shall be applied to the patients and epidemiological methods shall be used for the analysis of the data.

The CTD, like most Pharmaceutical legislation, has been adopted by the European Economic Area (EEA), which comprises of the countries (Member States) of the European Union as well as Iceland, Liechtenstein and Norway. Throughout this publication wherever reference is made to European Union/Member States it equally refers to these EEA countries.

Chapter 3 - Commencement of a Clinical Trial

Introduction

Prior to starting a clinical trial the sponsor must have obtained a favourable opinion from the Ethics Committee and received a Clinical Trial Authorisation (CTA) from the Competent Authority. The process of obtaining a CTA may be implicit whereby the Competent Authority has raised no objections to the application (formally referred to as "grounds for non-acceptance", or, for specific products (see Appendix 1) the CTA may be a written approval. Whilst the CTD guidance outlines the general processes to be followed, there are still important differences between the Member States with respect to both CTA and Ethics Committee applications. Specific national processes must be followed when making submissions. Contact details and web-site addresses of the Competent Authorities are listed within the guidance document[7].

Ethics Committees - General

The most significant statements made within the CTD with respect to Ethics Committees are as follows:

- Member States must establish and operate Ethics Committees, thus taking Ethics Committees into the legislative framework within each Member State. Prior to this the legal status of Ethics Committees varied across the European Union.

- For multi-centre research a single opinion must be given for each Member State involved, thus clarifying the situation when multiple Ethics Committees involved in a single clinical trial reach different opinions about the same study. However the CTD does not preclude an individual Ethics Committee from rejecting the study at an individual site without affecting the overall ethical approval status for that Member State.

- The timeframe for Ethics Committees to reach a decision has been set at a maximum of 60 days from the date of receipt of a valid application. Exceptions to this timeframe are envisaged with medicinal products for gene therapy/somatic cell therapy or genetically modified organisms, where a 30-day extension period may occur. If consultation with an external group or committee is required (per Member State laws) then a further 90-day extension may be permitted. Finally, for xenogenic cell therapy there is no time limit set in the CTD for the authorisation period. This reflects the complexity and seriousness of these therapeutic products.

- The Ethics Committees are only permitted to request supplementary information from the applicant on one occasion. Whilst the information is being provided, the 60-day review period is suspended, and restarts upon provision of the information.

- The Ethics Committee and Competent Authority applications may now run in parallel, whereas prior to the CTD many Member States required one of the approvals to be in place prior to making a submission to the other body.

Ethics Committee Objectives

To reach an opinion about a clinical trial the Ethics Committee is required to consider a number of areas, including the relevance of the clinical trial and clinical trial design; whether the anticipated benefits and risks are satisfactory; the protocol; the suitability of the investigator and supporting personnel; the quality of the facilities; the Investigator's Brochure and the adequacy of the written information sheets.

Ethics Committee Application – What information is required?

The document *"Detailed guidance on the application format and documentation to be submitted in an application for an Ethics Committee opinion on the clinical trial on medicinal products for human use[5]"* provides information related to the processes and format of applications to Ethics Committees.

Principles
- Everything given to the subject must be submitted to the Ethics Committee.

- Documents submitted to the Ethics Committees and the Competent Authority for consideration must be the same versions.

- All documents submitted to an Ethics Committee must be identified and version controlled.

- The applicant to Ethics Committees may be the sponsor or the Principal Investigator, dependent on national systems. Similarly the signatories on the application form should be the sponsor/sponsor's legal representative and/or the Principal Investigator at the site. For multi-site research it is expected that the co-ordinating investigator responsible for co-ordinating the Principal Investigators across the study within the Member State will sign the application form. In all instances national processes would take precedence.

- The Ethics Committee timelines start upon receipt of a valid application – with the first stage following receipt by an Ethics Committee being an administrative check that the information provided is complete. This is known as the 'validation check'. Following this check the applicant will be informed that the package is valid and the review period will start, or the applicant will be informed of the deficiencies. National processes should describe how Ethics Committees handle timelines with respect to this validation check of the package.

Application Content
The precise content of application to the Ethics Committee still varies between Member States; however the detailed guidance[5] describes the basic content required by the Member States and the processes that will be harmonized across the European Union.

All Member States require what is often referred to as the "basic package" of information (much of which is also required by the majority of Competent Authorities – see Competent Authority). It consists of the following:

- Covering letter (not required for Denmark)
- Application form, with EudraCT number
- List of Competent Authorities submitted to, with their decisions, where available
- Protocol
- Investigator's Brochure (or summary of product characteristics (SmPC for marketed products, according to sponsor wishes)
- Informed Consent Form/Subject Information Leaflet
- Arrangements for recruitment
- Insurance, indemnity and compensation information

The content and specifics of these are summarised below:

Application Form
The application form used will be in accordance with the Member State national procedures, but is expected to include the Clinical Trial Application Form used for Competent Authority submissions (see Competent Authority).

IMP information
The Application Form contains the information about IMPs used in the clinical trial, which, supplemented with the Investigator's Brochure or the summary of product characteristics (SmPC) for marketed products is usually sufficient for the majority of Ethics Committees. However, some Member States (for example, Greece and the Netherlands) have assigned responsibility for review of the Investigational Medicinal Product Dossier to the Ethics Committee. In these cases the full IMPD as described in the Competent Authority application must be submitted (see Competent Authority).

Protocol
The requirements with respect to the protocol for Ethics Committee applications are consistent with the Competent Authority requirements (See Competent Authority).

Some Ethics Committees require, in addition to the full protocol, a summary of the protocol in the national language. Member State procedures should be followed to meet this need.

Recruitment arrangements
The procedures for recruitment of patients should be described, either in the protocol or a separate document. The description of recruitment processes, as well as reasons for selection of patient groups should be provided. This is especially

important where patients are included who are not able to give informed consent.

If advertisements are planned to be used, then a copy of the materials <u>must</u> be provided to the Ethics Committee, including any printed material, recordings or videotapes. The plan for handling responses to the advertisements must be described, specifically outlining the process for handling patients who are not suitable for the study (e.g. referral to a treatment clinic).

The content and processes for advertisements must take into consideration any Member State legislation, but the guidance document contains the following points to consider including in an advertisement:

1. The research nature of the project

2. The scope of the trial

3. Which type/group of subjects might be included

4. The investigator clinically/scientifically responsible for the trial, if possible or required by local regulations

5. The person, name, address, organisation to contact for more information

6. That the subject responding to the advertisement will be registered

7. The procedure to contact the interested subjects

8. Any compensation for expenses

9. That a response on the part of a potential subject only signifies interest to obtain further information.

Subject Information and Informed Consent Procedures

The informed consent documentation and process is fundamental to protection of patients, therefore of specific concern to the Ethics Committee. The following points related to the informed consent process are selected from the guidance document as being particularly significant:

- All information to be provided to a potential subject before their decision to participate in a trial must be submitted to the Ethics Committee. The written informed consent form must also be provided.

- The information should be in compliance with ICH-GCP[6].

- There should be a description of planned arrangements for taking care of patients after their participation in the trial has ended, where there is additional care necessary because of the patient's participation in the trial and where it differs from that normally expected.

- The information sheets provided to the patients should be short, clear, relevant and understood by a layperson. They should be in a language known by the patient.

- If patients who are unable to give informed consent are included in the study, then different sets of informed consent documents will be required, to meet the needs of the legal representative and the patient (minor or incapacitated) as they will have different levels of understanding. The patient's information should include a statement that their decision not to participate or to withdraw from the study will be respected, even if consent is given by the parent/legal guardian. Here the detailed guidance document is not consistent with the CTD, which states that the patient's opinion will be 'considered'. Clearly any study involving these special groups requires careful planning and documentation on how these scenarios will be handled.

- A description of how of patient's personal data will be safeguarded is required in the patient information. This is described in the guidance as covering how the identity of the patient/subject, biological material obtained from the subject, and any recorded data will be coded, stored and protected. Furthermore information should be provided about the person(s) who will have access to the code list, where the code list will be kept, who is responsible for keeping it, and how long it will be retained. The information should address that the patient has the right to ask for updated information, to request corrections of errors and to know who will is responsible for keeping the data and who will have access. This represents significant detail about data processing and controls.

- A patient must be informed that they are able to withdraw their consent at any time and be able to request that previously retained identifiable samples will be destroyed to prevent future analysis, in accordance with any Member State rulings.

- The patient must be provided with a contact point where additional information can be about the trial, and the patient's rights, and whom to contact in the event of a trial-related injury occurring, again in accordance with the Member State ruling on this topic.

- The signature page of the informed consent form is described as containing three elements:

  - Consent to participate in the trial

  - Consent to make personal information available to the sponsor, their representatives, the regulatory authorities, and if applicable, the Ethics Committees

  - Consent to archive coded information, and for its transmission outside of the European Union, if applicable.

- In trials with patients who are unable to give informed consent the processes involved in obtaining consent/assent from the patient as well as consent from the legal representative should be described. Furthermore, in cases where a patient is unable to give consent but is able to form an opinion the plan for taking care of a difference of opinion between the patient and the legal representative about their participation in a study should be described.

- If the use of a witness is foreseen the procedure for selection and use of a witness should be described.

Suitability of investigator and facilities
The information included in the Ethics Committee submission should cover the following elements:

- The qualification of the principal investigator should be described in a current Curriculum Vitae (CV) and/or other documents. Any training in GCP as well as previous clinical trial experience should be described.

- Any conditions that might impact the impartiality of the investigator should be presented (e.g. financial conflict).

- As the Ethics Committee are required to provide an opinion about the suitability of the facilities to be used in the study a summary of these should be provided, for example, a statement from the head of the clinic/institution. Member States may have alternatives in place to satisfy this requirement.

Insurance and Indemnity
The provisions for insurance and indemnity to cover any injury or death of a patient should be described. In addition a statement should be made about the investigator and sponsor liabilities. In some Member States responsibility for reviewing this is transferred to the Competent Authority.

Financial Arrangements
The details on proposed financial transactions with the institution/investigator and patient/investigator compensation should be provided to the Ethics Committee. In some Member States responsibility for reviewing this is transferred to the Competent Authority.

Competent Authority Notification – General
The most significant statements made within the CTD with respect to initial notification to the Competent Authority are as follows:

- The sponsor must submit valid applications for authorisation to the Competent Authority in the Member State(s) in which the clinical trial is planned to be conducted.

- The Competent Authority has a maximum of 60 days to consider the application. Exceptions to the 60-day approval period are permitted for gene therapy/somatic cell therapy or genetically modified organisms, where a 30-day extension period may occur. For these products the 90-day period may also be extended for a further 90 days if consultation of a group or a committee is required, per local requirements of the Member State.

- For specific biotechnology and gene/cell therapy medicinal products described in Article 9 points 5 and 6 of the CTD (See Appendix 1) a written authorisation for the clinical trial will be issued to the applicant by the Member State. For all other medicinal product applications the Clinical Trial Authorisation will be implicit. However, it is stated that the Competent Authority may notify the applicant that there are no grounds for non-acceptance within the 60-day wait period. Much Member State legislation describes approval letters being issued within the 60-day review period, which is still within the requirements laid down in the CTD but does detract from the spirit of the implicit approval model.

- In the event of non-acceptance of the application by the Competent Authority the sponsor has only one opportunity to amend the application. If the amendment does not satisfy the Competent Authority then rejection will follow and the clinical trial may not begin in that Member State.

Competent Authority Application – What information is required?

The format and content of the initial application made to the Competent Authorities still varies across the European Union and is described within the *"Detailed guidance for the request for authorisation of a clinical trial on a medicinal product for human use to the competent authorities, notification of substantial amendments and declaration of the end of the trial"* [7]. In addition, the processes and other relevant application details are described.

The important aspects of this guidance are summarised below:

Initial Clinical Trial Application
The sponsor making the Clinical Trial Application is required to submit some general information about the clinical trial as well as study-specific documentation. The general information includes a list of all Competent Authorities to which the same application been already been submitted, together with their opinion if it is available. The opinion of any Ethics Committee(s) also has to be provided, and if, at any point, an Ethics Committee issues an unfavourable opinion then the applicant is required to update the Competent Authority and provide a copy of the unfavourable opinion. Finally, if the applicant is not the sponsor themselves, then a letter of authorisation from the sponsor must accompany the application. This authorisation is important because it assigns legal specific responsibilities for the clinical trial to the named organisation within the European Union. This is especially important when a sponsor does not have their own legal entity within the European Union.

Specific contents of the initial application to the Competent Authority are as follows:

Covering Letter
The application should include a signed and dated cover letter, this cover letter should contain within the header information

- The EudraCT number (see EudraCT)
- The sponsor protocol number
- The title of the clinical trial

The text of the letter should highlight any important issues about the clinical trial, such as any special populations planned to be included (e.g. minors / incapacitated adults); if the clinical trial represents a first in humans study or the medicinal products has unusual specification. Furthermore the cover letter should reference where in the application any additional details about the specific issue being highlighted can be found.

EudraCT Number

The EudraCT number must be quoted in the application and by the time the application is being submitted the full clinical trial details must have been entered into the EudraCT system. In addition, for the initial version of the EudraCT rolled out it is requested that a copy of the e-mail notification for the EudraCT registration step should be included in the application package.

Application Form

The Clinical Trial Application Form is accessed from the EudraCT database (see EudraCT). The information required within the form is study- specific and also Member State-specific. The applicant is required to complete the form and include a printed, signed and dated copy with the application together with an XML electronic copy of the application form provided on a disc.

According to the text within the guidance document (section 4.1.3) the signatory of the application form is attesting to:

- The information provided is complete
- The attached documents contain an accurate account of the information available
- In their opinion it is reasonable for the proposed clinical trial to be undertaken
- Any information provided to both the Competent Authority and the Ethics Committee is based on the same data

In addition, alongside the signature on the application form (section L) the applicant is attesting to the following:

- The information is correct
- The trial will be conducted according to the protocol, national regulation and the principles of good clinical practice
- It is reasonable for the proposed clinical trial to be undertaken
- A summary of the final study report will be submitted to the competent authority and the Ethics Committee concerned within a maximum of 1 year deadline after the end of the study in all countries
- The effective data of commencement of the trial (informed consent signature of the first patient) will be informed as soon as available to the concerned Authority and the Ethics Committees

Thus, in summary, the applicant of a clinical trial agrees to a number of very important responsibilities and logistical activities related to the conduct clinical trial.

The Protocol

The guidance document states that the content and format of the protocol must comply with ICH-GCP[6]. In addition, the version submitted must include all the approved amendments.

This guidance document continues to state that the protocol must also include:

- A definition of the end of the trial. In most cases this is expected to be the last visit of the last patient undergoing the trial. If there needs to be another definition assigned as the end of the trial then this should be described and justified in the protocol.

- An evaluation of the anticipated benefits and risks associated with the clinical trial.

- A justification for the inclusion of patient groups who are unable to give informed consent, or any other special patient populations.

- A description of the plan for any additional care to be provided to patients after the clinical trial has ended, where this differs from that normally expected according to the patient's medical condition.

Other guidance documents[8] state that

- The reference document (e.g. Investigator's Brochure or summary of product characteristics (SmPC)) against which expectedness of adverse reactions will be assessed should be stated in the protocol.

- If a product has several different SmPCs then the sponsor should state in the protocol which one will be used as the reference document for assessing expectedness of an adverse event.

The Investigator's Brochure

The guidance document states that the content, format and procedures for updating the Investigator's Brochure should comply with ICH-GCP[6]. The requirement within ICH-GCP for at least an annual review is probably the most problematic area. For marketed products it is anticipated that an extensive Investigator's Brochure may not be necessary, and the Investigational Medicinal Product Dossier (see below) may suffice.

The Investigational Medicinal Product Dossier (IMPD)

The IMPD provides summary information about the quality, safety and clinical use of all IMPs being used in the clinical trial, which includes any placebos and/or comparator products used. The IMPD also provides non-clinical data and a summary of the clinical use of the product(s) involved. The purpose of the IMPD is to provide sufficient detail about the products to allow the reviewer to reach a conclusion about the potential toxicity and safety of the product(s) proposed to be used in the clinical trial. Some of this information may already be presented within the Investigator's Brochure, in which case it may be cross-referenced, but there may be instances where a specific aspect of the data requires an additional discussion to be presented. In this case it should be contained within the IMPD.

Content of the IMPD

The IMPD should contain summaries of the quality, manufacture and control data related to the product(s) proposed for use in the clinical trial. It is recommended that wherever possible the organisation and layout of the data should correspond to the ICH Common Technical Document[9]. However, it is recognised that it may be inappropriate or impossible to provide all the information routinely included within the Common Technical Document. In general, the summaries should be tabular in format, provide a critical analysis of the data (not just raw data) and where applicable, reference other previous clinical trials.

The overall risk and benefit assessment of the clinical trial is an important section of the IMPD that critically analyses the non-clinical and clinical data relative to the potential risks and benefits of the proposed clinical trial. It should discuss the clinical relevance of any of the known non-clinical or clinical results and propose any further safety monitoring required in the clinical trial.

The guidance document presents scenarios when the full IMPD information may not be required, and a simplified IMPD can be prepared. The main scenarios when a simplified IMPD comes into use are as follows:

- The product has been assessed as part of a Marketing Application within any Member State or,

- The product has been part of a clinical trial application within a Member State or,

- Upon special agreement with the Competent Authority an adapted simplified IMPD may be appropriate

The content and format of the Simplified IMPD will depend on the previous data reviewed by the Competent Authority as part of the Marketing Authorisation or Clinical Trial Application and the status of any new data arising since the approvals. Appendix 2 summarises this.

Additional Applications before Initiating a Clinical Trial

This chapter has focussed on the applications required by the CTD 2001/20/EC[1] however, it must be remembered that there may be other additional applications and/or notifications required before a clinical trial can be started. These may be related to the specific products/medicinal products in use (for example compliance with the Directives 90/219/EC[10] and/or 2001/18/EC[11] may be required if a genetically modified organism is used within the IMP); also there will be national and/or local (or even site-specific) requirements that need to be fulfilled prior to starting the clinical trial.

Chapter 4 - During a Clinical Trial

Introduction

When a clinical trial is ongoing there will be a number of notifications required for submission to the Ethics Committee and the Competent Authority. These may include changes that a Sponsor chooses to make to the study / protocol and updating of information originally submitted about the study or IMP.

Substantial Amendments – General Information

Article 10 of the CTD describes how a clinical trial can be changed after it has started by means of an amendment. The most significant statements with respect to amendments are as follows:

- A substantial amendment that is likely to impact the safety of the trial subjects or to change the interpretation of the scientific documents supporting the clinical trial, or is otherwise significant, should be notified to the Competent Authority and the Ethics Committee(s) concerned. The content of, and reasons for the amendment must be provided.

- The Ethics Committee have a maximum of 35 days to provide their opinion to the applicant.

- The timeline for the Competent Authority review was not stated in the CTD but the guidance document[6] assumes a 35-day period to review and inform the applicant of any grounds for non-acceptance.

- If urgent safety information becomes available then the sponsor and the investigator must take appropriate urgent safety measures to protect the subjects against any immediate hazard. The sponsor shall then notify the Competent Authority and Ethics Committees of the new information and any measures taken with respect to the new information.

What is a Substantial Amendment?

A substantial amendment is described in the guidance document[7] as being a change to the study protocol or new information relating to the scientific documents that support the study where they are likely to have a significant impact on:

- The safety, physical or mental integrity of the subjects

- The scientific value of the trial

- The conduct or management of the trial or

- The quality or safety of the IMP used in the trial

Furthermore the guidance document provides examples of the types of changes that may be considered to be substantial amendments. These examples include changes to most sections of the protocol, changes in trial arrangements (including changes or additions to the investigators and CRO responsibility changes and changes to recruitment); changes to the IMP; changes to the non-clinical pharmacology / toxicology or changes to the clinical trial and human experience data which may affect the risk:benefit assessment. In summary, the changes that need to be treated as substantial amendments are much broader than just the protocol-specified details related to the conduct of the clinical trial.

How are routine substantial amendments reported?

The reporting process for substantial amendments will be determined by the urgency associated with the change. For routine substantial amendments the sponsor should report them using the Amendment Notification Form that is available from the EudraCT database. If the substantial amendment affects more that one study, which is likely to occur where the information about the IMP or other supportive data has changed, then the amendment notification can be made to cover several different studies. In this case the cover letter must clearly list all the clinical trials affected by the amendment and provide the EudraCT numbers.

How are emergency substantial amendments reported?

If the substantial amendment involves an urgent safety issue then the sponsor and the investigator must take whatever measures are required to protect the subjects against any immediate hazard. These urgent safety measures can be taken *without* the prior authorisation of the Competent Authority or Ethics Committee, *however*, the sponsor must inform the Competent Authority and Ethics Committee concerned of the new events, as well as the action plan as soon as possible. This initial notification in an emergency situation is expected to be via telephone followed by a written report. National procedures should be followed for these situations.

Interrupting a Clinical Trial – What needs to be done?

If a clinical trial is halted (e.g. recruitment and/or ongoing patient treatment is stopped) then the sponsor must notify the Competent Authority and Ethics Committee within 15 days using the Declaration of the End of a Trial Form.

It should be noted that the clinical trial cannot then be restarted until a favourable opinion of the Ethics Committee has been received and the Competent Authority have raised no grounds for non-acceptance for the recommencement of the trial. Thus, suspending a clinical trial is a significant step that should only be done when there is a real need as restarting the clinical trial is not a simple step, and it may have repercussions on the overall timeframes for completion of the clinical trial.

Who should substantial amendments be reported to?

The substantial amendment should be submitted to the group(s) that initially received the information that has changed, frequently this will be both the Ethics Committee and the Competent Authority. However, if the information was originally submitted to only one of these groups then when it is amended the other groups must still be informed that there has been a change made and submitted to the other group. So for example, if there is a substantial change related to the IMP data, which was not originally submitted to the Ethics Committee, when the amendment is submitted for approval to the Competent Authority, the Ethics Committee should also receive the same Amendment Notification Form informing them that a substantial amendment has been made to the Competent Authority regarding the IMP information. In this example approval is only being sought from the Competent Authority.

If a substantial amendment needs to be submitted to the Ethics Committee and the Competent Authority then this should be done in parallel with the same information being provided to both groups.

Substantial Amendments – What information is required?

The format and content of a substantial amendment to the Competent Authorities is described within the *"Detailed guidance for the request for authorisation of a clinical trial on a medicinal product for human use to the competent authorities, notification of substantial amendments and declaration of the end of the trial"*[7] and for the Ethics Committee within the *"Detailed guidance on the application format and documentation to be submitted in an application for an Ethics Committee opinion on the clinical trial on medicinal products for human use"*[5]. The content is very similar for both groups and summarised as follows:

Covering Letter
The application should include a signed and dated cover letter– this cover letter should contain within the header information

- The EudraCT number (see EudraCT)

- The sponsor protocol number

- The title of the clinical trial

The text of the letter should explain why the change is a substantial amendment and highlight any special issues about the amendment and state where the details can be found in the original application. Furthermore the cover letter should provide any other relevant information that is not included within the Notification of Amendment Form. If the applicant is not the sponsor then a letter of authorisation from the sponsor should be included with the amendment.

Notification of Amendment Form
The Notification of Amendment Form can be accessed from the EudraCT database and is used to submit the change to the Competent Authority and/or Ethics Committee for approval and/or notification purposes (see above).

Other Information to be provided with the Amendment

- Where the original data in the Clinical Trial Application Form (see CCTA) has been changed by the amendment then a revised version of the original Clinical

The Institute of Clinical Research

Trial Application form (XML file) should be provided together with a printed copy showing the changes highlighted.

- The modified documents, showing the content that has been changed. The previous and new wording, where applicable should be provided.

- New versions of the affected document. Where the changes require a new version of a document be produced then the new version should be submitted clearly identifying the updated number of the version and date.

- Any other supportive information relevant to the change. This could include, but is not limited to:

  - Summaries of data

  - Updated risk:benefit assessment

  - Possible consequences for subjects already included in the trial

  - Possible consequences on the evaluation of trial results

- In addition the Ethics Committee require explanation of the process to be used to obtain new consent from the patients using the updated information, where this is applicable.

When can a substantial amendment be implemented?

A routine substantial amendment can be implemented when there is a favourable opinion from the relevant Ethics Committee and there are no grounds for non-acceptance from the Competent Authority. If the substantial amendment has only been submitted to the Ethics Committee for approval then the sponsor may proceed when the Ethics Committee opinion is favourable. Similarly if the amendment only required to be submitted to the Competent Authority for authorisation then it may be implemented when no grounds for non-acceptance have been received from the Competent Authority. A maximum of 35 days are foreseen for these considerations, unless the Competent Authority require a consultative committee or group, in which case the sponsor should be notified of the extension to the timeline.

For timelines associated with the implementation of an emergency safety-related amendment (see Amendments).

Chapter 5 - End of a Clinical Trial

The end of a clinical trial must be defined in the protocol and in the majority of cases it will be the date of the last visit for the last patient. Furthermore if this definition changes then a substantial amendment must be prepared. The CTD states that the end of the clinical trial must be notified to the relevant Competent Authority and the Ethics Committee(s). The timelines for this notification vary depending on whether it is a routine end of a trial or a premature termination.

How is the end of a clinical trial notified?

The Declaration of the End of a Clinical Trial Form is used to notify the Competent Authority and Ethics Committee that a clinical trial has ended. This form is available from the EudraCT database (see EudraCT).

Routine end of a clinical trial

For a routine end to a clinical trial this form should be submitted when each Member State completes the study, and when the trial ends in all countries (including those outside of the European Union). The form should be submitted within 90 days of the last visit of the last patient. If the clinical trial has been short term and not subject to an annual safety report the CTD guidance recommends that the summary safety report be submitted with the end of the trial notification. This summary safety report should consist of at least the line listings, aggregate summary tables, if applicable and a statement on subject safety (see Subject Safety).

The sponsor is required to provide a summary of the clinical trial report within one year of ending the trial. This report summary should comply with the ICH guideline on Structure and Content of Clinical Study Reports[12]. The implication of this requirement is that provision of study results by the Sponsor to the Competent Authority (and the Ethics Committee) ensures that any potential public safety concerns are available external to the company and if warranted, could be further investigated by the Competent Authority. Previous allegations that sponsors had retained negative results of clinical trials within the company are clearly not possible in the new post-CTD environment.

Early termination of a clinical trial

For an early termination to a clinical trial the form must be submitted within 15 days and the following additional information should also be provided:

- An explanation and justification for the ending of the trial prematurely
- Number of patients still receiving treatment at the time of study termination
- Proposed management of patients still receiving treatment at the time of study termination
- Consequences for the evaluation of results

Post clinical trial events

Finally, even after the end of a clinical trial if any event occurs that is likely to have an impact on the risk:benefit assessment and could still impact the trial participants then the sponsor is required to notify the Competent Authority and Ethics Committees and inform them of a proposed action plan to ensure that patients are protected.

Chapter 6 – EudraCT Database

Introduction

One of the fundamental objectives of the CTD since its proposal was to enable clinical trial information to be shared amongst the Member States. The EudraCT database is the electronic tool that enables this to happen and from 1 May 2004 all clinical trials submitted to a Member State for a CTA are required to have a EudraCT number. The EudraCT number is an identification code obtained from the EudraCT database that is unique to a clinical trial, regardless of the number of Member States or clinical trial sites associated with the protocol.

The CTD laid down that the content of the EudraCT database would include the following:

- Extracts from the CTA and updates made to the initial application

- Substantial Amendment information

- Ethics Committee opinion

- Declaration of the end of a clinical trial

- Inspection information

The version of the EudraCT database rolled out for use from 1st May 2004 was referred to as "Lot 1" and it is foreseen that this will subsequently be replaced by another version. The supplementary guidance document[13] outlines the full content of the EudraCT database and the processes involved with its use. The official EudraCT website[14] also contains useful reference documents including an extensive User Manual which is available in multiple languages.

The summary information below refers to Lot 1 of the EudraCT database.

How is EudraCT accessed?

The EudraCT database is accessed via an Internet web browser using the URL http://eudract.emea.eu.int/ and many Competent Authority websites have links into the database. There are no special computer settings required for access to the database, although it is recommended to use Internet Explorer v5 or higher and a screen resolution of 1024 x 768. In addition, accessing the forms will require Adobe Acrobat reader (freely available) and MS Word.

When will EudraCT be used?

The EudraCT database will be accessed to request a EudraCT number, to enter information about the clinical trial into the database and to retrieve information (e.g. applications forms) used to make the necessary notifications for a clinical trial. These include the initial Clinical Trial Application Form, the Notification of Substantial Amendment Form, and the Declaration of the End of a Clinical Trial Form.

When must the information be entered into EudraCT?

The application for a EudraCT number can be made at any time point prior to the clinical trial application. If a sponsor would like to obtain the number early in their planning process, maybe when the full details about the clinical trial are not known, they can still access the EudraCT database and provide outline data to obtain the EudraCT number.However, as the EudraCT reference number includes a year identifier then it should be used within the same year it was obtained. Most importantly, if only outline information was entered into EudraCT to obtain the EudraCT number, the complete information must be entered into the database prior to submitting the clinical trial application.

To ensure compliance with the EudraCT database the following have been put in place:

- The Competent Authority and Ethics Committee applications will not be accepted if they do not have a EudraCT reference number stated.

- The validation check by the Competent Authority of the content of a Clinical Trial Application includes a review of the status of the EudraCT information, if it is incomplete, the Competent Authority will request that the database is updated or return the application.

During the conduct phase of a clinical trial any substantial amendments will require the applicant to access the EudraCT website and download the Notification of Amendment Form. This form is then completed and mailed as a signed hard copy together with other relevant documentation required for notification of a substantial amendment (see Substantial Amendment). This documentation includes a printed copy of the original Clinical Trial Application Form with the data changes relating to the substantial amendment highlighted.

At the end of a clinical trial the sponsor will be required to access the EudraCT database to obtain the Declaration at the End of a Clinical Trial Notification Form. This form is then completed and mailed as a signed hard copy, together with any other relevant documentation.

What information is in EudraCT?

For the Lot 1 version of EudraCT the information required in the database prior to submitting an application to the Competent Authority is a sub-set of the Clinical Trial Application information. It is detailed in the guidance documents[13] and summarised below:

Information required prior to submitting to a Competent Authority
A. Trial Identification

B. Identification of the Sponsor

C. Applicant Identification

D. Investigational Medicinal Product

E. Placebo

F. Release of IMP information

G. General information

H. Population of trial subjects

I. Proposed clinical trial sites

J. Ethics committee information

Following the Clinical Trial Application additional information is required within the EudraCT database. This is detailed in the guidance documents and summarised below:

Information completed by or after initiation
N. Review of initial application information

O. Amendments

P. Declaration of the end of the clinical trial

Finally, there is a sub-set of data that the Member State is required to enter into the EudraCT database. This is detailed in the guidance documents and summarised below:

Information completed by the Member State Inspectorate
Q. Inspection of clinical trial sites

R. Inspection of IMP manufacturer/importer

What language is used for the EudraCT database?
Data should be entered in English wherever possible, although the notification forms are being developed in other languages.

Who has access to data in the EudraCT database?
The applicant who entered the information into the database will have access to their information, but because the data is of a confidential nature access is strictly limited to the Member States, the Agency and the Commission. The CTD also states that if there is a substantiated request then the additional information submitted within the Clinical Trial Application, not routinely held in the EudraCT database, may also be released.

At the time this publication was being written there is a draft proposal from the European Commission to use information in the EudraCT database and make it publicly available[15]. Thus satisfying the requirement laid down in Regulation 726/2004[19] for transparency of information on clinical trials.

How will the EudraCT data be utilised?

The EudraCT database will hold information about all clinical trials being conducted, and completed, in the European Union. As the amount of data within the database increases the use of the data is expected to include the following:

- To provide an overview of all clinical trials within the Community.

- To facilitate communication between Member States (and the Agency and Commission) about clinical trials.

- To easily allow identification of clinical trials

  o related to a specific product / sponsor,

  o within a specific patient population,

  o by indication

  o by disease.

- To generate clinical trial statistics

- To interface with the Eudravigilance reporting processes

- To provide GCP and GMP inspection information

- To notify the Member States (Agency and Commission) when a clinical trial is terminated for safety reasons.

In summary, the EudraCT database provides the capability of accessing information related to ongoing and completed clinical trials within the European Union.

Chapter 7 – Adverse Event Reporting

Introduction

The CTD provides the legal basis for monitoring the safety of clinical trials such that if any clinical trial is deemed to pose an unacceptable risk it can be immediately stopped. The details within the CTD and associated guidance documents[8] cover Adverse Event (AE) and Serious Adverse Event (SAE) reporting, annual safety reporting requirements as well as introducing the Eudravigilance database[18]. These are covered in turn below.

Adverse Event and Serious Adverse Event Reporting

The highlights within the CTD related to reporting of AEs/SAEs are as follows:

- An investigator is required to report all SAEs immediately to the sponsor, except those identified in the protocol or Investigator's Brochure as not requiring immediate reporting.

- AEs and/or laboratory abnormalities identified in the protocol as critical to safety evaluations must be reported to the sponsor in accordance with the reporting requirements and as specified in the protocol.

- For subjects who die the investigator must supply the sponsor and Ethics Committee with additional information requested.

- The sponsor must keep detailed records of all SAEs.

The statements made in the CTD related to notification of SAEs are similar in nature to the ICH Clinical Safety Data Management guidelines,[16,17] such that:

- The sponsor must report suspected serious adverse reactions that are fatal or life-threatening as soon as possible to the Competent Authorities in all Member States concerned, and to the Ethics Committees, but in any case no later than 7 days of first knowledge by the sponsor.

- All other suspected serious adverse reactions shall be reported to the Competent Authorities concerned and the Ethics Committees as soon as possible but within a maximum of fifteen days of first knowledge.

- The Sponsor must inform all investigators.

Additional detail related to the definitions and processes for AE/SAE reporting are provided in the associated guidance document[8]. These are summarised below:

- The definitions relating to AE/SAE reporting are always important and the guidance document references the definitions within Article 2 of the CTD as well as the related ICH guidelines[16,17].

- The guidance document summarises the responsibilities of the investigator verbatim the CTD (as laid down in the first 3 bullet points at the beginning of this chapter) and then summarises that sponsors are responsible for:

- the ongoing safety evaluation of the IMP(s).

- the prompt notification to all concerned investigator(s), Ethics Committees and Competent Authority of findings that could adversely affect the health of subjects, impact on the conduct of the trial or alter the competent Authority's authorisation to continue the trial in accordance with Directive 2001/20/EC.

- arranging structures and written SOPs to ensure that the necessary quality standards are observed in every step of the case documentation, data collection, validation, evaluation, archiving and reporting.

Evaluation of AEs

The key evaluations required for AE/SAE reporting are those of seriousness, causality and expectedness.

Whereby:

A **serious adverse event** or reaction is defined in the CTD as any untoward medical occurrence or effect that at any dose resulting in death, is life-threatening, requires hospitalisation or prolongation of existing hospitalisation, results in persistent or significant disability or incapacity, or is a congenital anomaly or birth defect.

An **unexpected adverse reaction** is an adverse reaction, the nature and severity of which is not consistent with the applicable product information (e.g. Investigator's Brochure for an unauthorised investigational product or summary of product characteristics for an authorised product).

With a **causal relationship** being related to the definition of **adverse reaction**, which are defined as all untoward and unintended responses to an investigational medicinal product related to any dose administered.

Investigator and Sponsor Assessments

Individual events should be evaluated by the investigator for seriousness and causality and then reported to the sponsor for their evaluation. The sponsor evaluations include seriousness, causality and expectedness.

All cases judged by either the investigator or the sponsor as having reasonable suspected causality to an IMP qualify as an adverse reaction. The causality assessment of the investigator should not be downgraded, however if the sponsor disagrees with the investigator's assessment both opinions should be provided with the report.

Expedited Reporting of AEs

What needs to be reported?

All suspected adverse reactions related to the IMP (tested product and comparator)

occurring in a clinical trial, that are judged to be unexpected and serious (SUSARs) should be reported in an expedited manner. In addition for products that do not have a Marketing Authorisation in any Member State within the European Union the sponsor is required to report

- SUSARs from other trials occurring within or outside of the European Union

- Spontaneous or literature reports

- Reports transmitted to the sponsor by another regulatory authority

Initial Reports

For reporting purposes the electronic format described in the guidance associated with the Eudravigilance database[18] is preferred. However, at the time this publication was written the database was not fully implemented. The CIOMS-I form is the most widely accepted format for expedited reporting of AEs.

The minimum criteria for reporting AEs are:

- A suspected IMP

- An identifiable patient

- An AE assessed as 'serious' and 'unexpected' for which there is a reasonable suspected causal relationship

- An identifiable reporting source

- A unique EudraCT number (or for non-EC trials the sponsor's protocol number)

Follow-up Reports

If the initial report is incomplete at the time of the initial report all additional information should be sought. A Follow-up Report should then be made, stating any relevant additional information.

Confidentiality and Data Protection

When cases are reported the subjects' confidentiality must be protected. This includes compliance with Data Protection rulings. In AE/SAE management it is vital to ensure that no personal identifier information is erroneously included within the text fields of the report.

Reporting data from blinded clinical trials.

In general, the Competent Authority and Ethics Committee expect to receive unblinded SUSAR reports. The investigator should only break the code if the information is relevant for the safety of the patient. If the investigator has not broken the code, then the sponsor is expected to do this for reporting purposes, whilst still maintaining the blind for sponsor personnel involved in data management and analyses activities. This is to maintain the credibility of the blinding as far as possible.

High Morbidity and High Mortality Disease Clinical Trials

For high morbidity and high mortality disease clinical trials, where the efficacy end-points could be a SUSAR, or when a fatal or other life-threatening outcome could be a primary efficacy measure, the integrity of the clinical trial could be compromised if the blind are broken for these patients. Under these circumstances it is advisable to reach an agreement with the Competent Authority how the AEs related to the disease will be not subject to unblinding and expedited reporting. These agreements must be reached in advance of starting the clinical trial and the specific details about how reporting will be handled must be clearly described in the protocol. An independent Data Monitoring Committee (DMC) is then needed to oversee the trial and make decisions about any changes required, continuation or terminations. Opinions and decisions of the DMC should be reported to the relevant Competent Authority and Ethics Committee. Written procedures are needed to describe the operation of the DMC[6].

Expedited Reporting of Other Safety Information

In addition to AEs there may be other important safety-related data or information that requires expedited reporting to the competent Authority and Ethics Committee. These would include information that affects the risk:benefit assessment of an IMP (see IMP) or involve considering changes to the IMP administration or conduct of a clinical trial.

Some practical examples provided in the guidance document include:

- An increase in the rate of an expected serious adverse reaction that is judged to be clinically significant

- Post-study SUSAR reports that occur to a patient and are reported to the sponsor by an investigator

Format of non-AE Safety Expedited Reports

These reports should be made by letter with header information that it is a 'Safety Report'. The EudraCT number, protocol title and number should be included together with a summary of the points of concern raised in the report.

The Eudravigilance Database – Clinical Trial Module

In accordance with Article 24 of European Regulation EC No 726/2004[19] from 20th November 2005 all adverse drug reactions have to be transmitted electronically to the authorities. The Eudravigilance database was launched in December 2001 to meet this need, initially for post-marketed product reporting, and from 1 May 2004 for clinical trial reporting. The Eudravigilance data model is based on the requirements in the ICH Clinical Safety Data Management guideline[17]. In accordance with this guideline reports maybe submitted as XML messages or via web-based forms. However, at the time this publication was being written the Eudravigilance database was not fully implemented in the European Union. The details of the content and reporting processes are outlined in a guidance document[8].

Reporting rules

The following rules are set out to clarify the SUSAR reporting for sponsors of clinical trials.

- Sponsors who hold a marketing authorisation for at least one of the IMPs used in the study will report to either the post-marketing module (EVPM) or the clinical trial module of the Eudravigilance database (EVCTM).

- Sponsors who are not the marketing authorisation holder for any of the IMPs used in a study, will as a result of the reporting scenarios address all reports to the clinical EVCTM.

- As a general rule all SUSAR reports originating from any interventional clinical trial defined as being within the scope of the CTD, will send reports to EVCTM. This includes reports attributed to the comparator and placebo.

- To avoid double reporting any SUSAR case that is reported by the sponsor to a Member State according to the national legislation will not be forwarded by that Member State to the Eudravigilance database.

- Electronic reporting of SUSARS, with one or more investigators within the European Union should commence from 1 May 2004, regardless of the authorisation date for the clinical trial. However, retrospective reporting of SUSARs prior to the 1st May 2004 will not be required, and EudraCT numbers will not be required retrospectively.

Additional rules operate for sponsors who are also holding the Marketing Authorisation for a product that is an IMP in their clinical trial:

- SUSARS that originate from a non-EC country and that qualify as spontaneous reports in the country of origin, but the IMP does not have a marketing authorisation anywhere in the EC, will be reported to the EVCTM.

- SUSARS arising from any organised data collection system (other than interventional clinical trials) involving an IMP approved in at least one Member State will be submitted to the EVCTM. At the time of preparing this publication it was recognised that this may change in the future.

Annual Safety Reporting

The CTD requires that throughout the clinical trial the sponsor should provide, on an annual basis, to the Competent Authority and the Ethics Committee a listing of all suspected serious adverse reactions that have occurred over the period and a report of the subject's safety.

The associated guidance document[7] describes in more detail the content, format and processes associated with this annual safety reporting. These are summarised below:

Content of the Annual Safety Report
The annual safety report is made up of three parts

- A report of the subjects' safety in the clinical trial.

- A line listing of all suspected, serious adverse reactions that occurred in the clinical trial.

- An aggregate summary tabulation of suspected serious adverse reactions that occurred in the clinical trial.

A report of the subjects' safety in the clinical trial
This section contains the sponsor's analysis of the clinical trial, put into context the ongoing safety of subjects included in the clinical trial. It is a section of the annual safety report that requires significant effort to ensure that it provides the right level of critical analysis expected by the Competent Authority.

Specifically, the sponsor should prepare a 'concise' safety evaluation and risk: benefit evaluation of the clinical trial. This should provide any new information about the clinical trial or the IMP and critically evaluate the likely impact on the subjects in the clinical trial. 'New information' is defined as being that not already included in the Investigator's Brochure or the summary of product characteristics (SmPC).

An analysis of the implications on the patient population should also be provided together with an analysis of the safety profile of the IMP and the implications on subject exposure, in context of all the available safety data. The sub-sections recommended within this section include:

a) relation with dose, duration, time course of the treatment

b) reversibility

c) evidence of previously unidentified toxicity in the trial subjects

d) increased frequency of toxicity

e) overdose and its treatment

f) interactions or other associated risk factors

g) any specific safety issues related to special populations, such as the elderly, the children or any other at risk groups

h) positive and negative experiences during pregnancy and lactation

i) abuse

j) risks which might be associated with the investigation or diagnostic procedures of the clinical trial

Supportive non-clinical data should also be included, or any other experiences that provide information about the subjects' safety. Finally, a detailed rationale should be given stating whether it is necessary to amend the protocol, or other study documentation (informed consent documentation or Investigator's Brochure). If so, the usual amendment procedures should be followed (see Amendment of Protocol).

Line Listings

The line listings provide key data for the suspected adverse reactions occurring in the clinical trial.

Specific information provided in the guidance document related to the format and content of the line listings are as follows:

- A trial-specific line-listing of all suspected serious adverse reactions

- Key-data, but not necessarily all the information collected

- Each subject should be included only once, regardless of how many adverse reaction terms are reported. The case should be listed under the most serious, as judged by the sponsor. If a subject has different reports at different times, then these would be listed separately

- Cases should be tabulated by 'body system'

- The line listing should be referenced using the sponsor's reference number or date and time of printing

- In general there will be one listing per clinical trial, however, it may be separated by treatment groups

The specific data required for each subject in the line listing is as follows:

a) Clinical trial identification

b) Study subject identification number in the clinical trial

c) Case reference number in the sponsor's safety database

d) Country in which the case occurred

e) Age and sex of subject

f) Daily dose of IMP (and dosage form, route of administration, where appropriate)

g) Data of onset of the adverse reaction (if not known, best estimate of time to onset from therapy initiation. For an ADR known to occur after cessation of therapy, estimate of time lag, if possible)

h) Dates of treatment (if not available, best estimate of treatment duration)

i) Adverse reaction: description of reaction as reported, and when necessary as interpreted by the sponsor; where medically appropriate the signs and symptoms can be lumped into diagnoses, MedRA should be used

j) Patient's outcome (e.g. resolved, fatal, improved, sequelae, unknown). This field should indicate the consequences of the reaction(s) for the patient, using the worst of the different outcomes for multiple reactions

k) Comments, if relevant (e.g. causality assessment if the sponsor disagrees with the reporter; concomitant medications suspected to play a role in the reactions directly or indirectly; indication treated with suspect drug(s); dechallenge / rechallenge results, if available)

l) Unblinding results in the case of unblinded SUSARs Expectedness at the time of the occurrence of the suspected SARs, assessed with the reference document (i.e. Investigator's Brochure) in force at the beginning of the period covered by the report

Aggregate Summary Tabulations
The summary tables provide an overview of the adverse reactions across the clinical trial. However, if the number of cases is very small the overview might be best provided as a narrative description.

Where summary tables are prepared they should indicate the number of reports

a) for each body term

b) for each adverse reaction term

c) for each treatment arm, if applicable

The SUSARs should be clearly identified in the table.

Summary Annual Safety Reports
If there are several clinical trials ongoing with the same product a sponsor may decide to prepare a single annual report covering all the clinical trials. In this case the sponsor must provide reports from the anniversary of the first clinical trial authorisation until the end of the last clinical trial in any Member State. When one summary annual safety report is being prepared the sponsor is expected to include a global analysis of the IMP in relation to all the clinical trials and study populations, as well as the safety data for each clinical trial.

Timelines for Annual Safety Reporting
The timeline for the annual safety reporting is triggered by the date of the first Competent Authority authorisation of the clinical trial in any Member State. This date is designated as the cut-off date for data to be included in the annual safety report. The sponsor should submit the annual report within 60 days of the data lock point.

What if the product has a Marketing Authorisation?
If the product under test already has a Marketing Authorisation then the reporting period should be aligned with the International Birth Date of the product[20].

However, the Annual Safety Report and Periodic Safety Update Reports must remain as separate, stand-alone documents.

If during the clinical trial program a Marketing Authorisation is granted to the test product, then the reporting time frame for the IMP would become the International Birth Date.

Finally, if a clinical trial is short term (less than 6 months), then the safety report should be submitted within 90 days of the end of the trial when providing the End of Trial Notification to the Ethics Committee and Competent Authority (see Competent Authority). This report may be shorter, but should contain at least the line listings, aggregate summary tables, if appropriate, and a statement about the subjects' safety.

Reporting to Investigators

The sponsor is required to report to all investigators as soon as possible any findings that could impact the safety of study subjects or the course of the clinical study or development project. This can be achieved by providing individual AE and other relevant safety-related information and/or by providing line listings of SUSARs together with a summary of the evolving safety profile of the IMP. Where blinded clinical trials are ongoing it must be ensured that the investigators are not inadvertently unblinded and so if any line listings are provided the sponsor should ensure that the integrity of the blinding is maintained.

Post-study reporting requirements

After a clinical trial has ended any unexpected safety information that changes the risk:benefit assessment and is likely to impact subjects who have participated in the clinical trial should be reported to the Competent Authority. A proposed action plan should also be provided. This would include individual SUSARs reported by an investigator to the sponsor.

Chapter 8 - Investigational Medicinal Products

Introduction

Prior to the CTD the requirements for importation of IMPs differed between the Member States. Some countries required extensive and rigorous re-testing to import IMP into their boundaries, whereas others required much less or none. This situation was not felt to be beneficial to harmonise business across the European Union, nor to protect the European Union citizens. So, the CTD introduced a number of important requirements with respect to IMPs. These are summarised below:

- GMP principles must be applied to IMPs

- Manufacturing or importing an IMP requires an authorisation. The details of this authorisation are held in Member State legislation

- The holder of authorisation (see below) must have the services of a GMP Qualified Person available. The details of what is involved in being a GMP Qualified Person are as described in Directive 2001/83/EC[2] and 2003/94/EC[21]

- The GMP Qualified Person has specific duties and responsibilities including assuring that each batch of IMP has been manufactured and checked appropriately. This applies to test products, comparators and placebos, although the details of how this is assured will differ depending where the IMP is manufactured and whether the IMP has a marketing authorisation[22]. The GMP QP must also certify in a register, or equivalent, that each production batch satisfies the requirements

Additional guidance on IMPs is available in Annex 13 to Good Manufacturing Practice[22], which provides the requirements for manufacture, packaging, labelling of IMP to GMP principles. In addition, the Commission Directive on GCP[26] contains additional details about IMP manufacture/importation.

What does 'holder of authorisation' mean?

The legislation within each Member State defines what is needed to become an 'authorised' IMP manufacturer or importer. In the UK it requires obtaining a 'Manufacturer's Authorisation for Investigational Medicinal Product - MA(IMP)' for which there are specific application procedures to be followed.[23]

Scope of the IMP requirements

The requirements laid down in the CTD and Annex 13 to GMP applies to the manufacture and importation of IMPs. It is important to realise that the term 'manufacture' includes a wide range of activities including production, assembly, blinding and labelling of IMPs. Therefore, only an authorisation holder can perform these activities. Outside the scope of the manufacturing definition are dispensing and reconstitution activities, additional labelling of a product, and IMP activities related to individual patient supply for use within the institution[22]. In summary, great care must be taken to identify which activities are within the scope of these requirements, and to ensure only an appropriate authorisation holder performs these activities.

Profile of the GMP Qualified Person

The GMP Qualified Person is required to have specific qualifications and experience as defined in Directive 2001/83/EC[2] and must be identified on the Clinical Trial Application Form. The CTD laid down the opportunity for who were already performing the role for a specified time period, but not meeting all of the requirements laid down in 2001/83/EC to be assigned the role via a special transition process. Some Member States have also provided additional guidance for this transition process.

Labelling of IMP

The CTD laid down a requirement in Article 14 that the labelling used on the outer packaging of the IMP should be in at least the national languages(s) of the Member State. Annex 13 to GMP provides more detailed guidance on the labelling of IMPs, including a statement that the cumbersome details of the address and telephone number of the emergency contact to get more information about the clinical trial (e.g. for emergency unblinding) can be omitted if the subject has been given a leaflet or card which provides these details and the subject has been instructed to keep this in their possession at all times. This would need to be included in the documentation submitted as part of the study approval processes (See Chapter 3).

The Institute of Clinical Research

Chapter 9 – Regulatory Authority Inspections and Infringements

Introduction

Compliance with GMP and GCP is pivotal to implementation of the CTD, and Article 12 of the CTD outlines the grounds under which a clinical trial may be suspended or stopped by a Member State. In addition the CTD requires each Member State to appoint inspectors who will conduct inspections under their own procedures or those of the European Medicines Agency (EMEA).

These two aspects demonstrate the measures taken to ensure that the requirements of the CTD are enforced consistently across the European Union. In addition, the local legislation of each Member State may lay down the sanctions that will be taken for specific infringements of the clinical trial

What can be inspected?

Any facility involved in the clinical trial can be inspected, particularly the investigator sites, manufacturing sites, laboratories and sponsor sites. These inspections may take place within the European Union or in third countries outside of the EC.

How will inspections be conducted

The detailed guidance surrounding the inspectors and inspection procedures are not contained within the CTD, but are referenced as contained elsewhere. Detailed draft guidance documents were issued in 2002 describing the qualifications and training of inspectors[24] and inspection procedures[25] but these were never finalised, although some of the content re-appeared in the Commission Directive on GCP, issued in April 2005.[26]

What happens after the inspection?

Following an inspection the CTD states that an inspection report must be prepared which will be communicated to the sponsor, whilst maintaining confidentiality issues. It may also be made available to the other Member States, to the Ethics Committee and the EMEA, at their reasoned request.

Why could a clinical trial be suspended or stopped?

The Competent Authority have the right to suspend or stop a clinical trial if they have objective grounds to consider that the conditions laid down in the clinical trial authorisation are no longer being met, or there are doubts about the safety or scientific validity of the clinical trial.

Process for suspending or stopping a clinical trial?

Where the Competent Authority is considering suspending or stopping a clinical trial it shall, unless there is imminent risk, they will contact the sponsor and/or the investigator with the reasons for the proposed suspension/halting the trial and ask for their opinion. This opinion must be provided within one week.

Upon reaching a decision the Competent Authority will notify the other Competent Authorities, the Ethics Committees concerned, the EMEA and the Commission, stating the reason for the suspension/stopping the clinical trial.

Infringements

If a Competent Authority has objective grounds to consider that a sponsor or investigator, or any other person involved in the trial, is no longer meeting their obligations then they will write to the individual informing them of their infringement and indicate the course of action necessary to remedy the situation. Other Competent Authorities, Ethics Committees and the Commission will be informed. Upon receipt of this notification the sponsor is expected to immediately implement the course of action laid down in the action plan, and report back on progress and completion of the activities.

Chapter 10 - Protection of Subjects

Introduction

This chapter on protection of subjects has been purposely placed at the end of this publication because in fact, all aspects of the CTD directly, or indirectly enhance protection of subjects entered into clinical trials. The harmonised approaches to approval of clinical trials, including the increased focus on the risk:benefit assessments required to initiate a clinical trial, and to be continually monitored throughout the trial as more information becomes available. The requirement for clinical trials to be conducted using IMP that has been manufactured in accordance with GMP, and to conduct the trials in accordance with GCP, all contribute to enhanced patient protection. These newly harmonised standards for approving and monitoring clinical trials all increase the vigilance surrounding clinical trials.

In addition to these general measures of patient protection, there are specific requirements included in the CTD to ensure the protection of patients included in clinical trials, which are summarised below.

Protection of Subjects – General

- The CTD references the Declaration of Helsinki as providing the ethical basis for the conduct of clinical trials. Of note, the 1996[27] version is referenced in the CTD, even though the more controversial 2000[28] version was available at the time the CTD was published. This is a minor detail that should not detract from the intent, which is to ensure that the international standard for ethical conduct is embraced within the EC legislation. (The 2002[29] and 2004[30] clarifications have sought to reduce the controversy related to specific clauses within the Declaration of Helsinki 2000 version.)

- A statement is made that obsolete and repetitive testing should be avoided, either within the EC or outside in third countries. It is recommended that any available harmonised standards be followed, in particular the ICH guidelines, where possible. This helps ensure that subjects will not be recruited into poorly designed and/or conducted clinical trials where the resulting data cannot be used

- A clinical trial can only be initiated if the Ethics Committee and Competent Authority come to the conclusion that the anticipated therapeutic and public health benefit justifies the risks involved, and this risk:benefit relationship is permanently monitored

- All patients recruited into a clinical trial must understand the objectives, risks and inconveniences of the clinical trial, the conditions under which it will be conducted and that they have the right to withdraw from the trial at any time. This information must have been provided during the recruitment process by means of an interview held by the investigator (or a member of the team) prior to informed consent being obtained

- All patients must have given written informed consent (or used a legal representative, see below). If a patient is unable to write then oral consent in the presence of a witness may be used, as described in Member State legislation. This is described as being an exceptional circumstance

- Medical care and medical decisions being made during the clinical trial must be provided by an appropriately qualified doctor (or dentist, where appropriate)

- The subject must be provided with a contact point where they may obtain more information

- Insurance or indemnity provision must be in place to cover the liability of the investigator and the sponsor

Protection of Subjects – Confidentiality

Throughout the CTD reference is made to protecting the subject's rights to confidentiality of their data, and re-enforced by stating that compliance with the data protection Directive 95/46/EEC[31] is required, specifically with respect to processing of personal data and the free movement of personal data.

Protection of Subjects – Legal Consent

The first principle within the CTD is that subjects who are incapable of giving legal informed consent should only be included in clinical trials in restricted circumstances, where the results could not be obtained using persons capable of giving informed consent and there are grounds to consider that the direct benefit to the patient outweighs the risks. Furthermore, when these patients are included then special protection should be given. The CTD preamble requires the Member States to lay down rules for these instances, including the rules associated with the use of legal representatives. There are subsequent articles on two special groups included within this category, minors (Article 4) and incapacitated adults (Article 5) the details of which are summarised below.

Protection of Patients – Minors

Children are described as a vulnerable population with specific development, physiological and psychological needs, however, it is recognised there is a need to ensure that medicinal products that have been tested are available for this group of patients. This can only be achieved by studying medicinal products likely to be use in children. The overall objective is to ensure that clinical trials using children are specifically, designed, controlled and monitored to ensure the best protection possible for this group of vulnerable patients. Specific requirements include the following:

- Some direct benefit for the group of patients is obtained, and the research should either relate directly to a clinical condition from which the child suffers to be of such a nature that it can only be carried out on children.

- The clinical trial has been designed to minimise pain, discomfort, fear and any other foreseeable risk in relation to the disease, specifically the risk and distress thresholds have to be defined and constantly monitored

- The interests of the patient always prevail over those of science and society

- The relevant EMEA guidelines have been followed, this would include the ICH Guideline on Paediatric Clinical Trials[32]

- The Ethics Committee has endorsed the protocol, by using paediatric experts on their committee or seeking the advice of other relevant experts

- The informed consent of the parents (or legal representative) is obtained and this consent represents the presumed will of the child, and may be revoked without detriment to the minor

- The child must have been given information about the risks and benefits of the clinical trial according to the capacity of their understanding, and this information must have been provided using staff that are experienced with children

- If a child is capable of forming an opinion (e.g. an older child) and refuses to participate in a clinical trial then the wishes of the child must be considered by the investigator or principal investigator

- Financial inducement or incentives cannot be provided, except compensation (e.g. travel expenses)

The use of minors within a clinical trial should be highlighted in the Clinical Trial Application cover letter, as it represents a special population and is of significance to the review of the clinical trial by Competent Authorities and Ethics Committees.

Protection of Patients – Incapacitated Adults

Incapacitated adults are described as those patients who are incapable of giving their own consent to participate in a clinical trial. It includes patients with dementia, psychiatric conditions as well as more acute sever medical conditions (e.g. unconscious patients).

The requirements for persons incapable of giving informed consent include the following specific requirements are met:

- The research is essential to validate data obtained from clinical trials on patients able to give informed consent and relates directly to life-threatening or debilitating diseases, which the incapacitated adult suffers from

- It is expected that administering the medicinal product will produce a benefit that outweighs the risk, or there is no risk at all

- The clinical trial has been designed to minimise pain, discomfort, fear and any other foreseeable risk in relation to the disease, specifically the risk and distress thresholds have to be defined and constantly monitored

- The interests of the patient always prevail over those of science and society

- The Ethics Committee who reviewed the study endorsed the study after taking special consideration of the relevant disease and the patient population. They may have used a specialist already on their committee or taken other advice

- The informed consent of the legal representative has been obtained. This consent must represent the subject's presumed will, and may be revoked at any time

- The subject has received information about the clinical trial risks and benefits according to the capacity of their understanding

- If the subject is capable of forming an opinion, and they state that they do not wish to participate or wish to withdraw from a clinical trial, then this should be considered by the investigator or principal investigator

- Financial inducement or incentives cannot be provided, except compensation (e.g. travel expenses)

Again, the use of incapacitated adults within a clinical trial should be highlighted in the Clinical Trial Application cover letter, as it represents a special population and is of significance to the review of the clinical trial by Competent Authorities and Ethics Committees.

Appendix I

Medicinal Products requiring written authorisation from a Competent Authority to conduct the clinical trial[19]

Article 9, point 5:
Per Regulation 2309/93: Annex A; and now as described in Regulation 726/2004 Annex: part 1

Medicinal products developed by means of one or more of the following biotechnological processes:

- Recombinant DNA technology,

- Controlled expression of genes coding for the biologically active proteins in prokaryotes and eukaryotes including transformed mammalian cells,

- Hybridoma and monoclonal antibody methods.

Article 9. point 6:
Medicinal products for gene therapy, somatic cell therapy including xenogenic call therapy and all medicinal products containing genetically modified organisms.

Appendix 2:

Table 1: Reduced information requirements for IMPs known to the concerned competent authority[7]

Types of Previous Assessments	Quality Data	Non-clinical Data	Clinical Data
The IMP has a MA in any EU Member State and is used in the trial			
- Within the conditions of the SmPC	SmPC	SmPC	SmPC
- Outside the condition of the SmPC	SmPC	Yes (if appropriate)	Yes (if appropriate)
- With a change to the drug substance manufacture or manufacturer	S+P+A	SmPC*	SmPC
- After it has been blinded	P+A	SmPC	SmPC
Another pharmaceutical form or strength of the IMP has a MA in any EU Member State and:			
- The IMP is supplied by the MAH	P+A	Yes	Yes
The IMP has no MA in any EU Member State but drug substance is part of a product with a MA in a Member State and:			
- Is supplied from the same manufacturer	P+A	Yes	Yes
- Is supplied from another manufacturer	S+P+A	Yes	Yes
The IMP has a previous CTA in the Member State concerned**:			
- No new data available since CTA	No	No	No
- New data available since CTA	New Data	New Data	New data
The IMP is a placebo	P+A	No	No

* Where the change to the drug substance manufacture produces a new potentially toxic substance such as a new impurity or degradation product or introduces a new material in the production of a biological product, additional non-clinical information may be required.

** This may require a letter of authorisation to cross-reference to the data submitted by another applicant

The Institute of Clinical Research

References

Most of these documents are available free on the web.

- o Refer to the European Commission website http://pharmacos.eudra.org/ or the EUR-Lex website http://europa.eu.int/eur-lex/ for European Commission documents.

- o Refer to the European Medicines Agency website http://www.emea.eu.int/ for EMEA documents

- o Refer to the World Medical Association website http://www.wma.net/ for documents relating to the Declaration of Helsinki

The links to these references were correct at the time of print.

1. Directive 2001/20/EC of the European Parliament and of the Council of 4 April 2001 on the approximation of the laws, regulations and administrative provisions of the Member States relating to the implementation of good clinical practice in the conduct of clinical trials on medicinal products for human use. *Official Journal of the European Communities L121/34-44*

2. Directive 2001/83/EC of the European Parliament and of the Council of 6 November 2001 on the community code relating to medicinal products for human use. *Official Journal of the European Communities L311/67-128*

3. Directive 2004/27/EC of the European Parliament and of the Council of 31 March 2004 amending the directive 2001/83/EC on the Community code relating to medicinal products for human use. *Official Journal of the European Communities L136/34-57*

4. Directive 65/65/EEC of 26 January 1965 on the approximation of provisions laid down by law, regulation or administrative action relating to medicinal products. *Official Journal of the European Communities L22/369-373*

5. Detailed guidance on the application format and documentation to be submitted in an application for an Ethics Committee opinion on the clinical trial on medicinal products for human use. ENTR/CT2. European Commission, April 2004.

6. Note for Guidance on Good Clinical Practice. ICH Topic E6. CPMP/ICH/135/95. EMEA, May 1996.

7. Detailed guidance for the request for authorisation of a clinical trial on a medicinal product for human use to the competent authorities, notification of substantial amendments and declaration of the end of the trial. ENTR/CT1. European Commission, April 2004.

8. Detailed guidance on the collection, verification and presentation of adverse reaction reports arising from clinical trials on medicinal products for human use. ENTR/CT3. European Commission, April 2004.

9. Common Technical Document for the registration of Pharmaceuticals fir Human Use: Organisation of Common Technical Document. ICH M4Q. CPMP/ICH/2887/99. EMEA, February 2003.

10. Council Directive 90/219/EC of 23 April 1990 on the contained use of genetically modified micro-organisms. *Official Journal of the European Communities L117/1-14*

11. Directive 2001/18/EC of the European Parliament and of the Council of 6 November 2001 on the deliberate release into the environment of genetically modified organisms and repealing Council Directive 90/220/EEC, 31 May 2001. *Official Journal of the European Communities L106/1-39*

12. Note for Guidance on Structure and Content of Clinical Study Reports. E3. CPMP/ICH/137/95. EMEA December 1995.

13. Detailed Guidance on the European clinical trials database (EudraCT Database). ENTR/CT5.1, ENTR/CT5.2 and ENTR/CT5.3. European Commission, May 2004.

14. EudraCT website: http://eudract.emea.eu.int/

15. Draft –Guideline on the data fields from the European clinical trials database (EudraCT) that may be included in the European database on Medicinal Products. http://pharmacos.eudra.org/F2/pharmacos/docs/Doc2005/03_05/Draft_guid_EudraCT_data_20050303.pdf

16. Note for Guidance on Clinical Safety Data Management: Definitions and Standards for Expedited Reporting. ICH E2A. CPMP/ICH/377/95. EMEA, October 1994.

17. Note for Guidance on Clinical Safety Data Management: Data Elements for Transmission of Individual Case Safety Reports. ICH E2B. CPMP/ICH/287/95 modification. EMEA, November 2000.

18. Detailed guidance on the European database of suspected Unexpected Serious Adverse Reactions (Eudravigilance – Clinical Trial Module). ENTR/CT4. European Commission, April 2004.

19. Regulation (EC) No. 726/2004 of the European Parliament and the Council of 31 March 2004 laying down Community procedures for the authorisation and supervision of medicinal products for human and veterinary use and establishing a European Medicines Agency. *Official Journal of the European Communities L136/1-33*

20. Note for Guidance on Clinical Safety Data Management: Periodic Safety Update Reports for Marketed Drugs. ICH E2C. CPMP/ICH/288/95. EMEA, December 1996.

21. Commission Directive 2003/94/EC of 8 October 2003 laying down the principles and guidelines of good manufacturing practice in respect of medicinal products for human use and investigational medicinal products for human use. *Official Journal of the European Communities L262/22-26*

22. Volume 4 Good manufacturing practices Annex 13. Manufacture of investigational medicinal products. European Commission, July 2003. http: //pharmacos.eudra.org/F2/eudralex/vol-4/pdfs-en/anx13en.pdf

23. Medicines for Human Use (Clinical Trials) Regulation 2004. SI 2004 (No. 1031), HMSO, 2004.

24. Draft – Detailed guidelines on the qualifications of inspectors who should verify compliance in clinical trials with the provisions of good clinical practice for an investigational medicinal product. European Commission, 2002. http: //pharmacos.eudra.org/F2/pharmacos/docs/Doc2002/june/ins_gcp_06_2002.pdf

25. Draft – Detailed guidelines on inspection procedures for the verification of GCP compliance. European Commission, 2002. http://pharmacos.eudra.org/F2/ pharmacos/docs/Doc2002/june/dtld_06_2002.p df

26. Commission Directive 2005/28/EC Laying down principles and detailed guidelines for good clinical practice as regards investigational medicinal products for human use, as well as the requirements for authorisation of the manufacturing or importation of such products. European Commission, 2005. *Official Journal of the European Communities L91/13-19*

27. World Medical Association Declaration of Helsinki Ethical Principles for Medical Research Involving Human Subjects, South Africa 1996.

28. World Medical Association Declaration of Helsinki Ethical Principles for Medical Research Involving Human Subjects, Edinburgh 2000.

29. World Medical Association Declaration of Helsinki Ethical Principles for Medical Research Involving Human Subjects, Edinburgh 2000. Note of clarification on paragraph 29 added by the WMA General Assembly, Washington 2002.

30. 200 World Medical Association Declaration of Helsinki Ethical Principles for Medical Research Involving Human Subjects, Edinburgh 2000. Note of clarification on paragraph 30 added by the WMA General Assembly, Tokyo 2004.

31. Directive 95/46/EC of the European Parliament and of the Council of 24 October 1995 on the protection of individuals with regard to the processing of personal data and on the free movement of such data. *Official Journal of the European Communities L281/31-50*

32. Note for Guidance on Clinical Investigation of Medicinal Products in the Paediatric Population. ICH E11. CPMP/ICH/2711/99. EMEA, July 2000.

Index

M

Manufacturer's Authorisation Investigational
  Medicinal Product 35
Multi-centre Research 6

N

National Legislation 2
Notifications 16
Notification Amendment Form 18

O

Objectives of CTD 2

P

Patient's personal data 10
Patient information 9
Post Clinical Trial Events 21
Protection of Patients 39–42
  - Confidentiality 40
  - Incapacitated Adults 41
  - Legal Consent 40
  - Minors 40
Protocol 8, 14, 20, 26, 29
Protocol Amendments. *See* Substantial
  Amendments

R

Recruitment of Patients 8

S

Safety evaluation 31
Scope of CTD 5
Serious Adverse Event or SAE 27
SmPC 8, 14, 31, 44
Substantial Amendments 16–18
  - emergency 17
  - information required 18
  - routine 17
Summary Annual Safety Reports 33

V

Validation of Applications 7